Goddess
RISING

Goddess RISING

Soulful connection to empower and unleash
your inner Goddess to rise above and see beyond

NIKKI TEGG

the kind press

Copyright © 2020 Nikki Tegg

First published by the kind press, 2020

All rights reserved. No part of this book may be reproduced, stored in a retrieval system or transmitted in any form or by any means, electronic, mechanical photocopying, recording, or otherwise, without written permission from the author and publisher.

This book is written as a source of spiritual guidance only. The advice and information in this book should not be considered a substitute for the advice of a qualified medical professional or registered psychologist. The author and the publisher expressly disclaim responsibility for any adverse effects arising from the use or application of the advice and information in this book.

Illustrations by Suzzi Hartery
Cover design and typeset by Elle Lynn

Cataloguing-in-Publication entry is available from the National Library Australia.

NATIONAL LIBRARY OF AUSTRALIA

ISBN 978-0-6488706-5-4 (Paperback)
ISBN 978-0-6488706-6-1 (ebook)

With love and gratitude to my family. You are forever my world. Thank you from the bottom of my heart and soul for your support, love and unwavering, unconditional love. You ground me, inspire me to soar and to reach my dreams.

With love and gratitude to my soul sisters. Our sacred sisterhood circle is strong!

And to your sacred sisterhood circle, wherever you are in the world, may you connect, love, create magick and heal together.

I've always being inspired and connected to the moon, the sky, the stars, always fascinated! And as I've grown that love has expanded even more.

I have re-learned, re-discovered, re-membered, re-ignited the knowledge of the Goddess and re-connected with my inner wisdom. I invite you to take the journey as well.

With love, light and magick,

Nikki Tegg

Psychic, Medium, Reiki Healer, Sacred Space Holder, Intuitive Writer; Creatrix

You are rising, sweet soul
You are loved unconditionally
You are embraced
You are held
You are seen
You are heard
You are here
You are magickal
You are perfectly imperfect
You are worthy
You are re-ignited
You are paving a new way
You are rising, sweet soul

Discover your inner Goddess.

Empower your warrior.

They have been with you all along.

They are ready to break free...

And so are you.

Ignite your Goddess

Let your

inner Goddess

meet your

inner Warrior…

Wouldn't that be kick arse?

Your life will never be the same.

Glow

What a beautiful sight, to glow with the moon.

It speaks to her so deeply and her soul responds.

She feels its constant pull.

She surrendered and unwound the ties of passed learned lessons that held her back.

She listened to her intuition and her heart lead the way.

She surrendered and danced under the shimmer of the midnight sky. The gleam of moonbeams shone on her as she moved across the stage of the Universe.

Inspire *Love*

Manifest *Growth*

Inspire *Reflection*

Manifest *Change*

Inspire *Release*

Manifest *Renew*

Inspire *Self Love*

Manifest *Beyond*

Inspire *Your Soul*

Spirit

Your inner power within fuels your strength.

Your strength embodies your femininity.

Your femininity builds your flow.

Your flow transfers to your creativity.

Your creativity inspires your dreams.

Your dreams inspire your manifestations.

Your manifestation sparks your inner power.

And your inner power ignites your spirit.

Cosmos

With magick in her veins and
The cosmos in her heart,
She shone for all to see.
The moon sang to her and
The sun helped her grow.
She wasn't afraid to be.
Her alchemy is within us
It illuminates the night.
She is a child of the Universe.
She owns her light.
She is permitted to be free.
To let live and to love.
The power to Be.

She turned inward and
whispered to herself,
'I love you', 'I accept you,'
and 'I am ready to shine'.

The Veil

She could always see the veil.

It was transparent.

She lived, waiting for someone to realise who she really was, to break down her façade she fought so hard to keep.

She felt like an imposter, an actor playing out her life rather than immersing herself in the root of her life.

She was exhausted.

Who she is was buried underneath the expectations from herself, as a child, as a teenager, as a naïve young woman, as a sensual being.

She lifted the veil that separated herself from her authenticity in search of the hands of her sisters that would mould and shape her future self.

She walked through and embraced the shadow.

She tore through the binding constraints to turn and face the light.

She released and let go.

And she shone.

My Journey

*I am the creatrix of my story.
I reflect on my past and manifest my dreams
for my life.*

The Sacred Circle

They sat in full circle.

Not one leader,

But all leaders.

No hierarchy,

But all respected.

They shared vulnerability,

Not knowing others' path or reason.

They connected hands.

They connected love.

They connected spirit.

They left on a journey.

Soaring through the sky with goddesses and guides.

Touching stars, crinkling the sky, leaving streams in their wake.

They returned.

Sharing an understanding, a knowing,

Yes.

This is their circle.

They adjusted each others crowns.

They are soul sisters.

Igniting Moon Magick

Beginning Moon

Stars luminous against the inky black sky.

The new moon is reborn and waiting.

The opportunity to refresh, relinquish and renew is upon you.

Manifest authentic intentions, the moon and Universe will hear your whispers.

They have been observing your shift.

Be abundant with gratefulness.

Use this moment with purpose.

Embrace the lessons and lean into them with your divine heart.

Take time to flow.

Move with intention and let your intuition steer you on your path.

Manifest, release, reflect and flow.

You are held in the arms of the moon.

Leap of Faith

She walks along the shoreline as the waves kiss her feet.

She wears the night as a cloak.

She is unafraid as this is her sanctuary.

She converses with the goddesses,

they bring her guidance.

She gives them love, trust and

is completely uninhibited.

Her inner knowing is shining through.

Now, she will be her own beacon of light,

for she knows only her heart, her mind, her spirit.

She's ready to take a leap of faith and she will fly.

Extend your arms,
let your wings be seen.
For today is a magnificent day,
to carry on your dreams.

They have been observing your shift, your guides, ancestors and goddesses. Accept, release, trust and completely surrender in in the divine timing of the Universe.

Manifest with the New Moon

New Moon Magick

Goddess:

Crone Goddess of the Triple Goddess. She is the wise woman, guide, counsellor, infinite teacher.

Crystals:

Moonstone
The moon's stone, harmonising, protection, fertility.

Labradorite
Higher connection, higher consciousness, magick, boost intuition.

Citrine
Manifestation, happiness, light.

Clear quartz
Clarity, manifestation, focus.

Rituals:

- Write out a manifestation
- Set new intentions for moon cycle
- Journal
- New moon bath

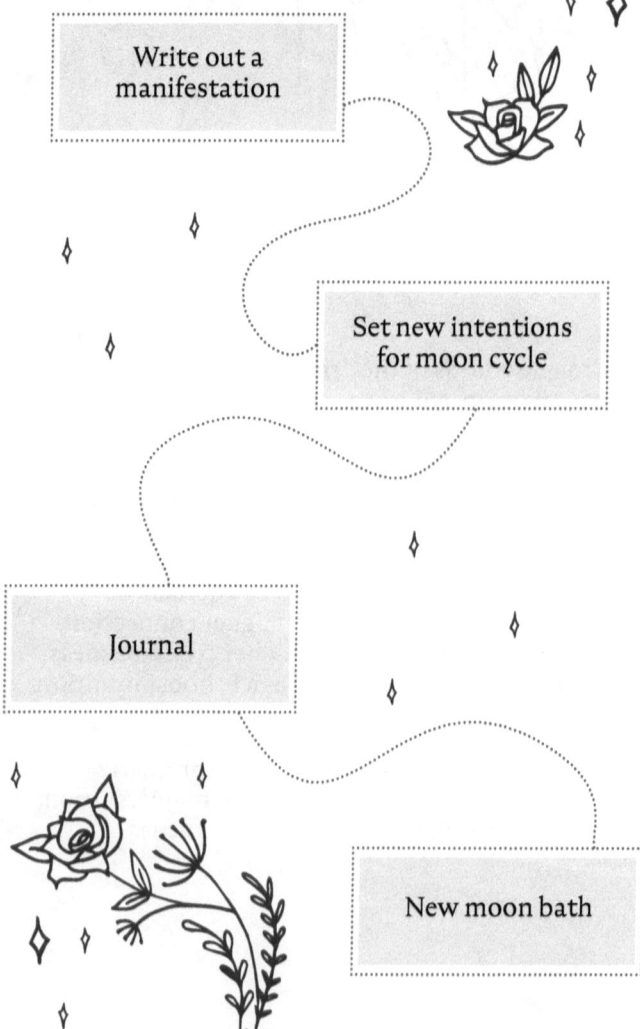

- Smudge and cleanse room/house
- Create a sacred space, setup a new moon altar
- Draw an oracle card or reading
- Meditate
- Create a vision board

Moon Spell: New Moon

I bathe in her night and surrender to her beams, I shine my inner light and manifest my dreams.

Create a space, just for yourself, play your favourite calming music and set the intention to manifest. Select crystals if you are called to amplify your energy. With your hand on your heart, find your centre. Just sit in your space feeling your heart beating. Take a deep breath, and on your inhale, feel your breath expand within your body. On your exhale let everything go that does not need to be present right now, in this moment. Reflect upon your journey and where you are on your path at this time. Visualise all the wonderful possibilities that you would love to bring into your life. Be clear and precise. With a grateful heart, give thanks for all that's in your life, the lessons and the blessings.

New Moon Manifestation

Tonight, I call to the moon, to hear my dreams and call forward my manifestations with a loving, grateful heart

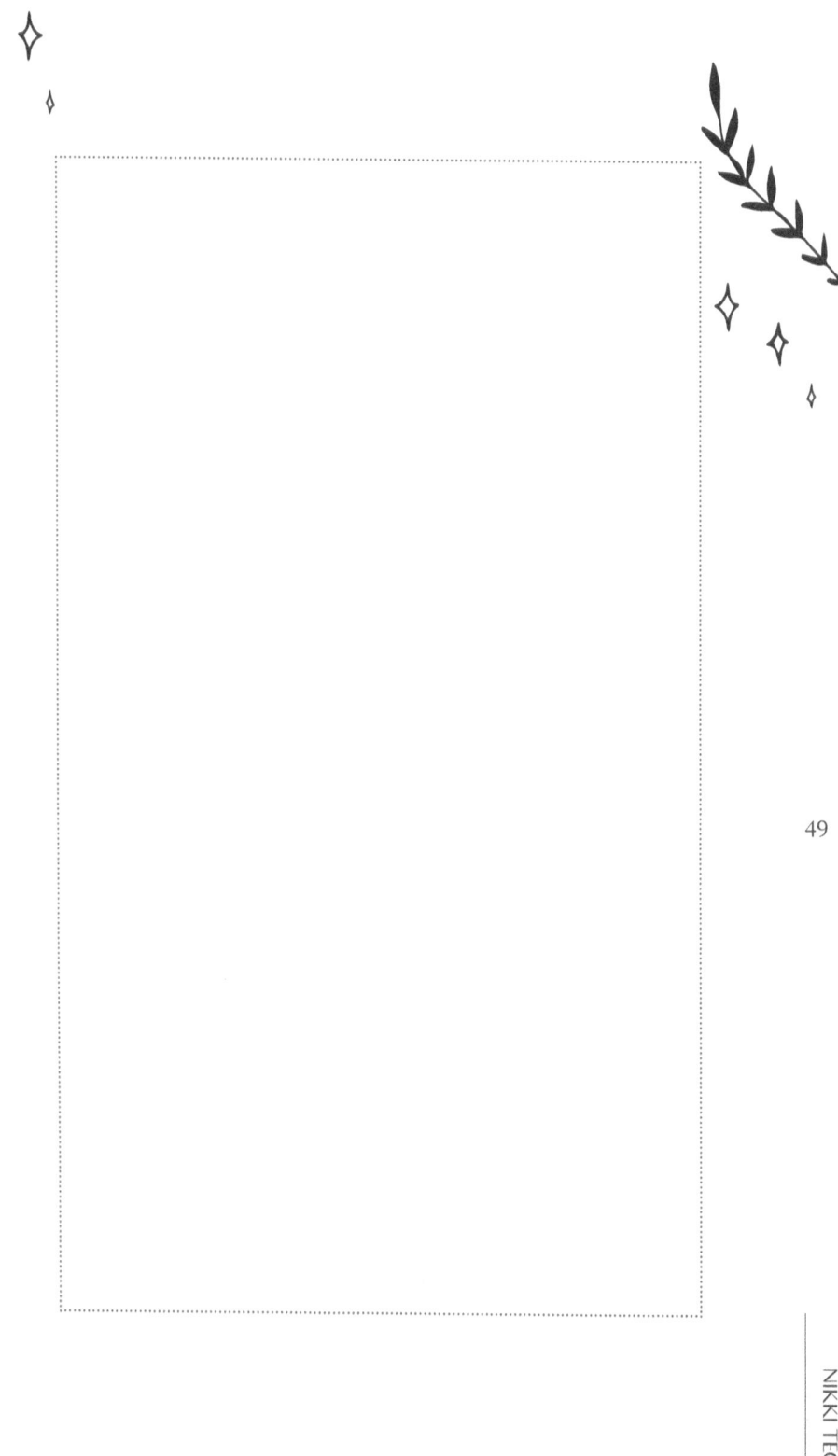

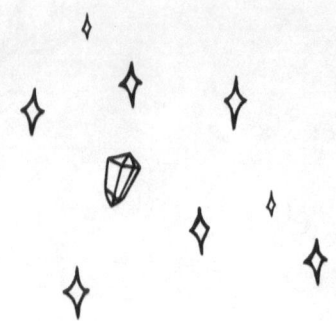

Channel

Her vibe is high and sets the atmosphere with pure intentions.

She is at one with herself.

She flies with the goddesses and greets them with open arms.

She walks with the spirits, her guides and embraces them lovingly.

She embodies the earth and connects with the maiden, the mother and the crone.

She is love.

In all its purity.

Re-member...

You're a woman.

The power of your magick is within you.

Universe

The cobblestones of your awakening cling together to prepare you on your new path. They are stable. They rise to meet your steps.

They won't let you fall.

The Universe has your back as you transform and change and grow.

It won't let you fall.

The Goddess has plans for you, even though they may not be the plans you thought of.

She won't let you fall.

She believes in you; She always has, and She always will.

She won't let you fall.

Woman

Be the woman who stands in her power.

Be the woman who re-members.

Be the woman who intently manifests.

Be the woman who loves herself.

Be the woman who stands with friends.

Be the woman who empowers authenticity.

Be the woman who causes change.

Be the woman who moves mountains.

Be the woman who values others.

Be the woman who creates magick.

Be the woman who embodies compassion.

Be the woman who listens.

Be the woman who dances in the wind.

Be the woman who uses her voice.

Be the woman who is raw, real, wild and free.

Be the woman that you are.

Rising

You are rising.

Plant your feet into the earth and feel it breathe and move within.

Embrace your Goddess within; She is awake, stirring and invoking your power within.

Embrace your feminine energy, as it is wild and ready to burst through.

Speak your truth, unbind your voice.

You are an empowered warrior.

Let your wild woman roar.

Listen to the world.

Hear with your heart.

Feel with your body.

Send loving vibrations out into the world, let your soul light the way.

Sacred New Moon Meditation

I invite you to become comfortable in your space. Know that you are safe and ready to take a journey with the new moon. Take a beautiful cleansing breath in, filling your lungs, and let that breath out, let it flow from you with love. Inhale and on the out breath let go of anything that is occupying your mind at this time. Right here is where you need to be. Feel the tension, stress, tightness leaving your body.

Imagine in your mind/feel in your body/know in your heart, beautiful streams of ribbon leaving your feet and moving through the Earth, past your earth star chakra, (which is located about six inches below your feet), winding and finding its way to the centre of the earth where a beautiful crystal is glowing, pulsating. Imagine in your mind/feel in your body/know in your heart, your ribbons wrap and plait themselves around the crystal. Through your ribbons you feel the pulse of the Earth, know that you are ground here. The pulse travels along your ribbons into your body illuminating each chakra as it moves. Your root chakra (at the base of your spine), sacral chakra (in your womb space, below your belly button), solar plexus chakra (above your belly button, where your diaphragm is) to your heart chakra. Here, place your hand on your heart and feel it pulsating, rest here for a moment, feeling the beating and pulse of your heart. The pulse travels to your throat chakra (at your neck), to your third eye chakra (between your eyebrows), opening the eye widely and to the crown chakra (just above your head). Feel the Earths' pulse travel up and burst through your soul star chakra (located six inches above your head), emanating silvery shimmery light into the Universe. Feel its connection with you.

You find yourself at the top of hill. The land around you is cleared except for lush grass moving in the slight warm breeze. It is after dusk; you can still see all the way to the horizon and beyond. Above you the inky navy sky is infinite. You lay down, gazing into the sky above. You catch, just a glimpse of the beautiful, still new moon, so dark and full of ancient wisdom and secrets of the Universe.

As your eyes relax you notice beautiful stars starting to fill the space above. Each one revealing itself in divine timing.

They glisten and shine so wonderfully, clustering together to form galaxies. As you're admiring the art of the stars, you notice ribbons of colours bending and moving together throughout the atmosphere. You reach up to the sky because need to touch the colours of pure light. As you do, the ribbons gravitate to your hands, blues, green, pinks, purples, silver, gold. You close your eyes and you begin to move your hands in a graceful rhythmic dance, weaving your magick, your love and your intentions into the sky. They lift you up to the moon. You stand on the moons' surface. You feel the energy Moon Goddess presence. She is listening and watching your intentions and manifestations that you have set yourself, that you want to bring into your life. She is singing to you, weaving her own magick, igniting your own inner wisdom. Your body sways, twirls, turns and moves with the music of the moon. The Moon Goddess, as She is your Crone, appears in divine feminine form. She reaches for you and embraces you in a beautiful embrace. She holds the ancient wisdoms of the Universe and she gifts you with the knowledge that you need. You stay together to share your manifestations.

It is time for the Moon Goddess to say farewell to you, but before She does, She tells

you that she is always watching and you can always call on her. The ribbons slowly lower you back down to the top of the hill, where you began. The ribbons roll up into ball that balances in the palms of your hands. It glows so beautifully, and it becomes a solid shining sphere. You place the sphere to your heart space and the light shines from within yourself.

As you lay back down to watch the stars, you notice that they begin to disappear back into the inky night sky. You are being called to return home. You feel the pulsation of the earths crystal slowly beginning to unwind itself. Imagine/see/feel your ribbons in the earth travel back down through the dirt, through your earth star chakra back into your feet. Start to feel the environment around you, feel your chair or bed underneath you. Know that you are back in your sacred space, safe and content. Start to wiggle your toes and fingers and slowly open your eyes when you are ready.

Welcome back.

Sacred Reflections

Rebirth

As the branches birth new foliage and open themselves to new possibilities.

I too renew, refresh and release.

I smile.

I feel.

I crave.

I stand.

I dance.

And meet the seasons of my life with a grateful heart.

Release with the Full Moon

Full Moon Magick

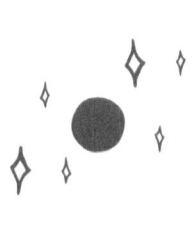

Goddess:

Mother Goddess of the Triple Goddess-nurturer, carer, midwife, womanhood guide.

Crystals:

Moonstone
Harmonising, protection, fertility.

Selenite
Cleansing, healing, protection.

Smoky quartz
Grounding, release, transmutation.

Celestite
Releasing, uplifting, calming.

Aquamarine
Tranquillity, peace, release.

Rituals:

Write down on a piece of paper what you would like to release. Be specific and feel it deeply within. Safely burn it and release the feelings held within

Shower by candlelight, imagining the water releasing and cleansing

Journal

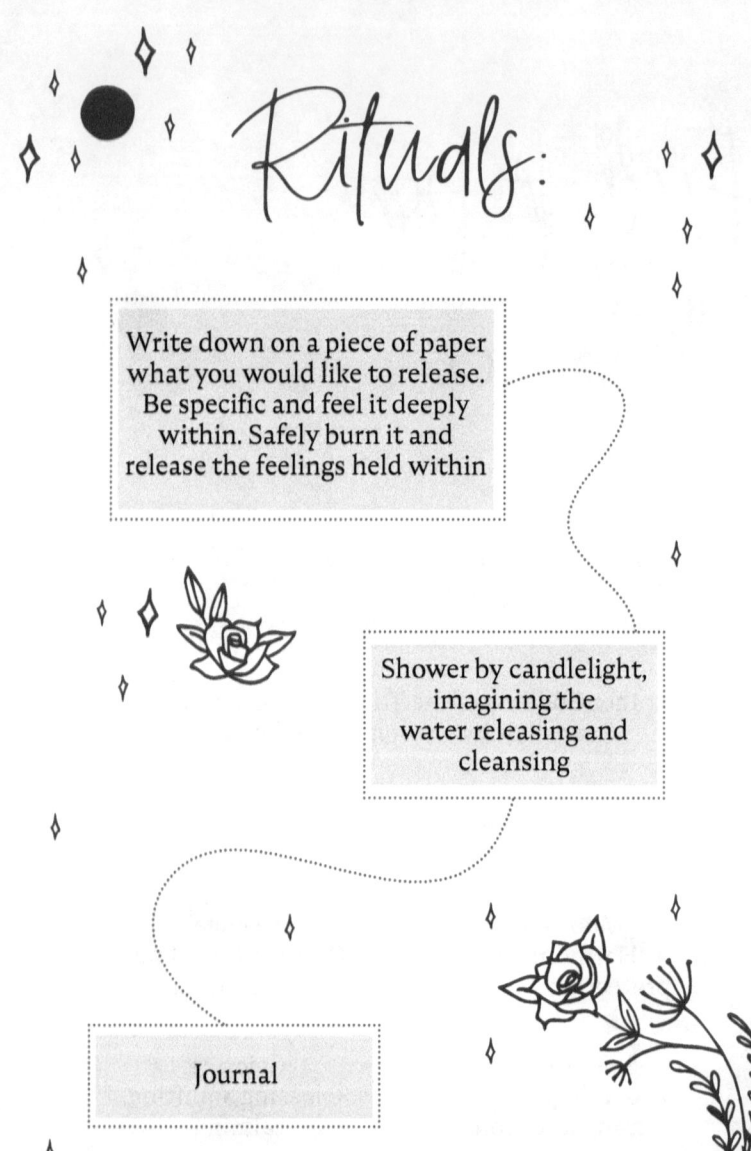

Charge crystals, outside in the moon light. Can place in dirt or on a natural surface

Make moon water, infused with rosemary

Create

Set sacred space

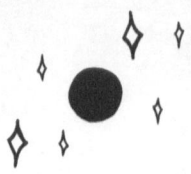

Moon Spell: Full Moon

I dance in her beams and become in tuned, I can forever be myself and release with the moon.

Oh! Full moon, how I do love you! Well, all phases of the moon if I am honest. Releasing with the full moon is powerful, can be emotional and rejuvenating. Take a deep breath and sit in your sacred space with any emotions, fears, notice any stirrings within that no longer serve you. It can be a habit, a toxic relationship, a change that isn't fulfilling you. Then, poised with a pen, write it out. Write out all the 'stuff' that no longer serves you. Get it out. Be specific in what you are releasing and tell it to the moon. Write it out, then burn it baby! (Safely.) Exhale a beautiful breath and let it go.

Tonight, I release to the moon, what is holding me back; my fears, self-doubt, my emotions and attachments that no longer serve me.

I call to the moon to clear my path with a cleansing heart.

Full Moon Release

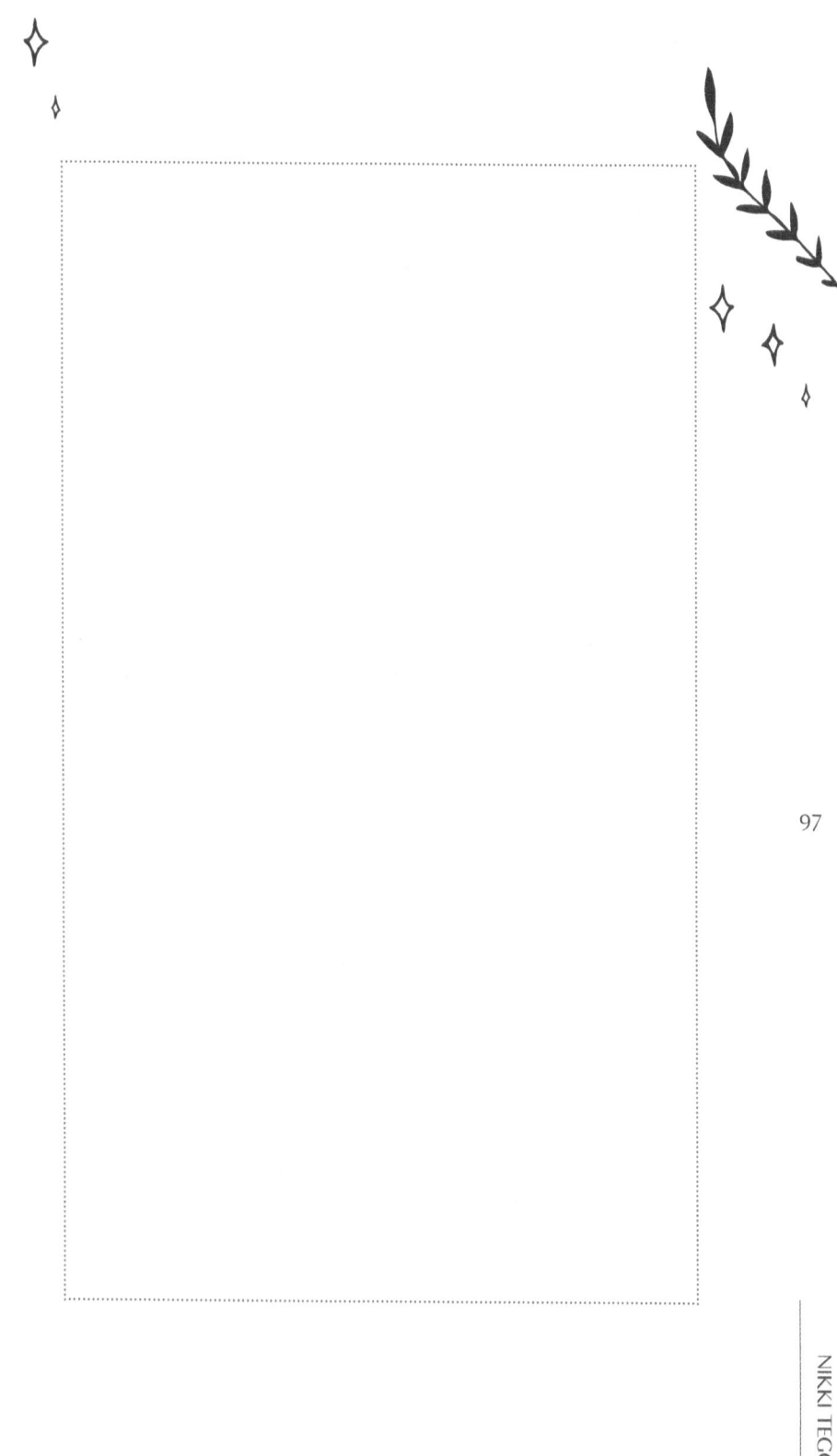

I am a moon lover, star gazer, earth hugger, magick weaver, storyteller, laugh out loud, creatrix, soul sister, take no shit, woman of the Universe.

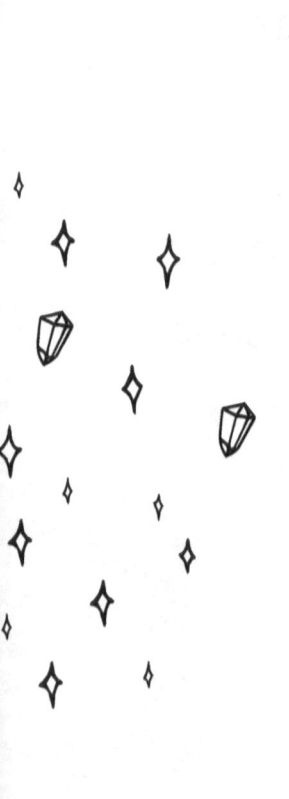

Ready

She stood poised.

She is graceful.

She is feminine.

She is focused.

She is fire.

She is flow.

She is warrior.

She is open.

She is grounded.

She is connected.

And. She. Is. Ready.

My Time

My heart feels content as I have walked this path before.

My feet brush over the warm crushed granite beneath them.

My nose fills with aromas of autumn.

My body feels your glow.

My heart beats to your call, your warmth radiates with such force.

There you are, standing gracefully where two paths diverge.

We stand face-to-face, hand in hand. No words uttered.

We have met before, you know me to the depths of my soul, my shadows, my light.

You share your wisdom. I do not question. I choose my path.

I glance back from where I began. I take a deep breath and step with intent.

My time is now.

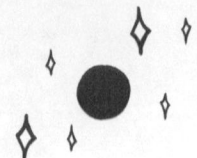

Inner knowing

She was captivated by the warmth of the sun.

She turned to face the rays and allowed the heat to fill her up from the inside out.

She is a fighter.

She knows this will pass.

She stands tall as one but knows that her soul sisters and ancestors have her back as she travels on her journey, guiding her from within.

You are on a new journey.

Embrace the steps that you are taking.

They are giant leaps of faith.

It's working.

Let it flow.

Frozen

On the outside, it was freezing;
The wind kissed her
skin with icy lips.

On the inside, it was
warm, comforting, loving
unconditionally.

The wind danced with her hair.

She felt playful and in perfect
balance with Mother Earth.

She had felt this longing
to strip away to
her bare, raw self.

She ran with a new-found courage,
breaking barriers and seeing
herself in a new light.

She danced with the wind and
beamed.

The path you're taking doesn't always lead to the place you thought.

It leads you somewhere better.

Breathe

Take a sip, drink it in; close your eyes.

Take a moment ... breathe.

Let the warmth emanate within your body.

You reflect upon what you are grateful for.

You embrace that feeling; you open your eyes.

Let the warmth surround your body.

You want to smile more, hug more, and love more.

Let the warmth flow from your body.

A Moment

Close your eyes.

Breathe deeply.

Breakthrough all your walls that protect your heart from the world.

Open your eyes.

Breathe deeply.

I see you, as you see me.

You are so worthy.

Let. That. Shit. Go.

Let your heart sing and
your soul reign.

Surrendering

Surrender
to the rain as it cleanses and refreshes.

Surrender
to the fire as it releases and renews.

Surrender
to the wind as it carries and expands your breath.

Surrender
to the earth as it grounds and clings to your roots.

Surrender
And be guided by your intuition and the universal call.

Rise above,

                see beyond.

Rise above,

love within.

Full Moon Release

A meditation with the Welsh Triple Goddess Cerridwen

I invite to you to be comfortable in your space. To extend and feel the space around you. To know deep within that you are held, safe, loved, supported and guided from within and from your guides.

Imagine in your mind/feel in your body/ know in your heart a beautiful glowing sphere of light just above your crown chakra. Imagine in your mind/feel in your body/know in your heart the colour of this beautiful warming light. It glows with the wisdom of the Goddess, wisdom of the Universe. It floats down through you crown chakra and as it enters your chakra you feel the warmth flow through your body. It illuminates each chakra as it passes, third eye, throat, heart, solar plexus, sacral, root, right down to your feet, its energy places your feet firmly into the earth. You feel the dirt beneath your feet. Here, imagine in your mind/feel in your body know in your heart beautiful roots grounding you, burrowing through the Earth to the centre, where the roots wrap themselves around a pulsating crystal. Feel the energy of the crystal and the earth, traveling up the roots back into your body. Feel it move quicker now, through your chakras and burst through your crown chakra connecting you to oneness of the Universe. Feel the energy vibrating around you.

Imagine in your mind/feel in your body/know in your heart you are walking down a gravel, clay road. The road is lined with soft grasses and flowers that move gently in the warm breeze. It is evening, and on the horizon, the last glow of the sun descends. You feel safe and a belonging in your heart that this path is where you need to be right at this moment. You pass fields of wildflowers, which fill up the space with their vibrant colours.

You notice that trees begin lining the road and see that they are getting taller and taller as you stroll along. You have ventured far along the road and the trees make a beautiful archway, a tunnel that you are travelling through. As you walk, up ahead you see a woman, beckoning for you to come to her. She looks very familiar to you, but just can't place it. She embraces you and joins you on your path and as you walk hand in hand, she is so pleased you are here tonight as it is an important step in your journey. You arrive at beautiful cottage. It has a thatched roof, planter boxes on the windowsills, flowers and herbs growing surrounding the cottage. Here is the Goddess Cerridwen's, cottage (Triple

Goddess, keeper of the sacred cauldron). Tonight, you lead the way and you hold the door for the woman to enter, she enters. The cottage smells of all the wonderful aromas of magick. You pass through the sitting room, where a warm inviting fire is burning, and enter the magickal kitchen where herbs are drying, candles alight with enticing scents, crystals lining benches.

It's good to be in this potent sacred space, feeling the warmth and sense of belonging within. In the kitchen, you see Cerridwen standing at the large table. She is adding and mixing ingredients into her large copper cauldron. She beckons you forward to help her get the potion ready. You ask her what she needs you to do but she replies by giving you a soft smile and saying, 'You'll know, trust your inner wisdom'. The three of you, spend time, collaborating together and adding the last remaining ingredients. Cerridwen and the woman both announce that the moon is ready, and it is now the best time for the release ritual. The three of you work together in taking the cauldron out back to the sacred garden. You place the cauldron into position, directly under the full moon above. The moon is so large and bright it feels as if you can reach out and grab it. The stars are aglow and dancing through the sky. Cerridwen says that it's now time for the final piece of the ritual – your release. You reach into your pocket and pull out a piece of paper with your release message you have written down on it so intently. As you recite what you have written, you tear it up and put it in the cauldron. She hands you a glass of liquid from the cauldron and invites you to drink. You do and it's the perfect drink for you, you feel it flow through your body.

You are free from what no longer serves you; you are free from what holds you back; you are free from limiting beliefs. You join hands with Cerridwen and the woman, who now you have come to realise is your higher self, to bring the for the power of 3. You feel your body let go of what no longer serves you. As the sacred 3, you spend time here together, listening, connecting, sharing the magick together.

You feel like it is time to go, and say farewell, leaving Cerridwen and head back through the cottage with love, confidence and sisterhood in your heart, knowing that you three create something so potent and magickal here that you are always welcomed back.

You enjoy the feeling that is flowing within and from you as you walk, with the full moon leading you back. The trees begin to thin and shorten. The grass and wildflowers appear in the fields and along the road and you are back where your journey began.

You know that you hold sacred knowledge within. You imagine in your mind/feel in your

body/know in your heart that your roots are unfurling from the crystal at the centre of the Earth. Feel them travel back to the soles of your feet. Visualise holding your sphere of light in front of you and place it in your heart. Start slowly wriggling your feet, hands, slow moments in your body.

Welcome back.

Sacred Reflections

I love myself enough to know that my self-care is about me. It is nobody else's business. It's not selfish, it's replenishing my mind, body, soul and spirit. I check in with myself, to realign my centre and to give back to me. I am worth it.

My self-care rituals

**What nourishes my soul?
What can I do to take time and give back to myself?**

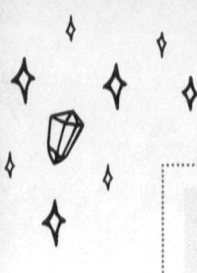

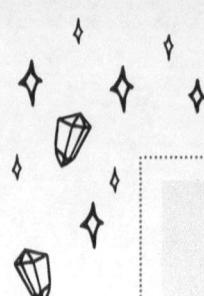

She Ran

She ran.

She ran so fast the wind couldn't catch her.

She sped through the atmosphere and leapt into the abyss.

There was nothing to catch her except her knowing that the Universe surrounds her and will propel her forward through the new world.

What calls you?

Is it your intuition?
Trust your inner voice, it will guide you.

Is it your home?
Go to your home, rest and renew.

Is it the ocean?
Become weightless in the ocean, go with the flow.

Is it the earth?
Seep into the earth and ground yourself.

Is it the wind?
Dance with the wind, move freely and breathe deeply.

Is it your heart?
Answer your heart desires.

Is it your light?
Embrace your light, shine and release.

Is it your inner child?
Play with your inner child, set her free.

Is it the fire within?
Ignite the fire within and feel the passion.

Is it the wild woman?
Welcome the wild woman for she knows you.

Live it, love it, feel it.
Be the authentic you.

Step lightly.

Step with intent.

Step with purpose.

Step with love and magick in your heart.

Mapping My Moon

It has always pulled my curiosity to see how my cycle syncs with the moon. There are also spiritual connections when flowing with the moon. If you have your moon time when it's the new moon you may feel more connected to your intuition and if it's the full moon, you may feel inspired to create. I take note of the moon phases and how my body is feeling and how I'm travelling emotionally. I invite you to explore and find how you feel during your moon time.

To map your moon, start at the beginning of your moon time by noting the moon phase. Notice over time how it changes.

Feel into the flow of the moon, take note when your body needs to rest, move, feeling sensual, be productive, create, practise self-care or retreat. Start at any time as the days are not dated.

Happy mapping.

Mapping my Moon

I move through my cycle with flow;
I feel my connections with the phases of the moon

Sunday	Monday	Tuesday	Wednesday	Thursday	Friday	Saturday
Date:	Date:	Date:	Date:	Date:	Date:	Date:
Moon Phase: ○	Moon Phase: ○	Moon Phase: ○	Moon Phase: ○	Moon Phase: ○	Moon Phase: ○	Moon Phase: ○
Cycle Day:	Cycle Day:	Cycle Day:	Cycle Day:	Cycle Day:	Cycle Day:	Cycle Day:
Date:	Date:	Date:	Date:	Date:	Date:	Date:
Moon Phase: ○	Moon Phase: ○	Moon Phase: ○	Moon Phase: ○	Moon Phase: ○	Moon Phase: ○	Moon Phase: ○
Cycle Day:	Cycle Day:	Cycle Day:	Cycle Day:	Cycle Day:	Cycle Day:	Cycle Day:
Date:	Date:	Date:	Date:	Date:	Date:	Date:
Moon Phase: ○	Moon Phase: ○	Moon Phase: ○	Moon Phase: ○	Moon Phase: ○	Moon Phase: ○	Moon Phase: ○
Cycle Day:	Cycle Day:	Cycle Day:	Cycle Day:	Cycle Day:	Cycle Day:	Cycle Day:
Date:	Date:	Date:	Date:	Date:	Date:	Date:
Moon Phase: ○	Moon Phase: ○	Moon Phase: ○	Moon Phase: ○	Moon Phase: ○	Moon Phase: ○	Moon Phase: ○
Cycle Day:	Cycle Day:	Cycle Day:	Cycle Day:	Cycle Day:	Cycle Day:	Cycle Day:
Date:	Date:	Date:	Date:	Date:	Date:	Date:
Moon Phase: ○	Moon Phase: ○	Moon Phase: ○	Moon Phase: ○	Moon Phase: ○	Moon Phase: ○	Moon Phase: ○
Cycle Day:	Cycle Day:	Cycle Day:	Cycle Day:	Cycle Day:	Cycle Day:	Cycle Day:

Mapping my Moon

I move through my cycle with flow;
I feel my connections with the phases of the moon

Sunday	Monday	Tuesday	Wednesday	Thursday	Friday	Saturday
Date: Moon Phase: ◯ Cycle Day:	Date: Moon Phase: ◯ Cycle Day:	Date: Moon Phase: ◯ Cycle Day:	Date: Moon Phase: ◯ Cycle Day:	Date: Moon Phase: ◯ Cycle Day:	Date: Moon Phase: ◯ Cycle Day:	Date: Moon Phase: ◯ Cycle Day:
Date: Moon Phase: ◯ Cycle Day:	Date: Moon Phase: ◯ Cycle Day:	Date: Moon Phase: ◯ Cycle Day:	Date: Moon Phase: ◯ Cycle Day:	Date: Moon Phase: ◯ Cycle Day:	Date: Moon Phase: ◯ Cycle Day:	Date: Moon Phase: ◯ Cycle Day:
Date: Moon Phase: ◯ Cycle Day:	Date: Moon Phase: ◯ Cycle Day:	Date: Moon Phase: ◯ Cycle Day:	Date: Moon Phase: ◯ Cycle Day:	Date: Moon Phase: ◯ Cycle Day:	Date: Moon Phase: ◯ Cycle Day:	Date: Moon Phase: ◯ Cycle Day:
Date: Moon Phase: ◯ Cycle Day:	Date: Moon Phase: ◯ Cycle Day:	Date: Moon Phase: ◯ Cycle Day:	Date: Moon Phase: ◯ Cycle Day:	Date: Moon Phase: ◯ Cycle Day:	Date: Moon Phase: ◯ Cycle Day:	Date: Moon Phase: ◯ Cycle Day:
Date: Moon Phase: ◯ Cycle Day:	Date: Moon Phase: ◯ Cycle Day:	Date: Moon Phase: ◯ Cycle Day:	Date: Moon Phase: ◯ Cycle Day:	Date: Moon Phase: ◯ Cycle Day:	Date: Moon Phase: ◯ Cycle Day:	Date: Moon Phase: ◯ Cycle Day:

Mapping my Moon

I move through my cycle with flow;
I feel my connections with the phases of the moon

Sunday	Monday	Tuesday	Wednesday	Thursday	Friday	Saturday
Date:	Date:	Date:	Date:	Date:	Date:	Date:
Moon Phase: ○	Moon Phase: ○	Moon Phase: ○	Moon Phase: ○	Moon Phase: ○	Moon Phase: ○	Moon Phase: ○
Cycle Day:	Cycle Day:	Cycle Day:	Cycle Day:	Cycle Day:	Cycle Day:	Cycle Day:
Date:	Date:	Date:	Date:	Date:	Date:	Date:
Moon Phase: ○	Moon Phase: ○	Moon Phase: ○	Moon Phase: ○	Moon Phase: ○	Moon Phase: ○	Moon Phase: ○
Cycle Day:	Cycle Day:	Cycle Day:	Cycle Day:	Cycle Day:	Cycle Day:	Cycle Day:
Date:	Date:	Date:	Date:	Date:	Date:	Date:
Moon Phase: ○	Moon Phase: ○	Moon Phase: ○	Moon Phase: ○	Moon Phase: ○	Moon Phase: ○	Moon Phase: ○
Cycle Day:	Cycle Day:	Cycle Day:	Cycle Day:	Cycle Day:	Cycle Day:	Cycle Day:
Date:	Date:	Date:	Date:	Date:	Date:	Date:
Moon Phase: ○	Moon Phase: ○	Moon Phase: ○	Moon Phase: ○	Moon Phase: ○	Moon Phase: ○	Moon Phase: ○
Cycle Day:	Cycle Day:	Cycle Day:	Cycle Day:	Cycle Day:	Cycle Day:	Cycle Day:
Date:	Date:	Date:	Date:	Date:	Date:	Date:
Moon Phase: ○	Moon Phase: ○	Moon Phase: ○	Moon Phase: ○	Moon Phase: ○	Moon Phase: ○	Moon Phase: ○
Cycle Day:	Cycle Day:	Cycle Day:	Cycle Day:	Cycle Day:	Cycle Day:	Cycle Day:

Mapping my Moon

I move through my cycle with flow;
I feel my connections with the phases of the moon

Sunday	Monday	Tuesday	Wednesday	Thursday	Friday	Saturday
Date:	Date:	Date:	Date:	Date:	Date:	Date:
Moon Phase: ◯ Cycle Day:	Moon Phase: ◯ Cycle Day:	Moon Phase: ◯ Cycle Day:	Moon Phase: ◯ Cycle Day:	Moon Phase: ◯ Cycle Day:	Moon Phase: ◯ Cycle Day:	Moon Phase: ◯ Cycle Day:
Date:	Date:	Date:	Date:	Date:	Date:	Date:
Moon Phase: ◯ Cycle Day:	Moon Phase: ◯ Cycle Day:	Moon Phase: ◯ Cycle Day:	Moon Phase: ◯ Cycle Day:	Moon Phase: ◯ Cycle Day:	Moon Phase: ◯ Cycle Day:	Moon Phase: ◯ Cycle Day:
Date:	Date:	Date:	Date:	Date:	Date:	Date:
Moon Phase: ◯ Cycle Day:	Moon Phase: ◯ Cycle Day:	Moon Phase: ◯ Cycle Day:	Moon Phase: ◯ Cycle Day:	Moon Phase: ◯ Cycle Day:	Moon Phase: ◯ Cycle Day:	Moon Phase: ◯ Cycle Day:
Date:	Date:	Date:	Date:	Date:	Date:	Date:
Moon Phase: ◯ Cycle Day:	Moon Phase: ◯ Cycle Day:	Moon Phase: ◯ Cycle Day:	Moon Phase: ◯ Cycle Day:	Moon Phase: ◯ Cycle Day:	Moon Phase: ◯ Cycle Day:	Moon Phase: ◯ Cycle Day:
Date:	Date:	Date:	Date:	Date:	Date:	Date:
Moon Phase: ◯ Cycle Day:	Moon Phase: ◯ Cycle Day:	Moon Phase: ◯ Cycle Day:	Moon Phase: ◯ Cycle Day:	Moon Phase: ◯ Cycle Day:	Moon Phase: ◯ Cycle Day:	Moon Phase: ◯ Cycle Day:

Mapping my Moon

I move through my cycle with flow;
I feel my connections with the phases of the moon

Sunday	Monday	Tuesday	Wednesday	Thursday	Friday	Saturday
Date:	Date:	Date:	Date:	Date:	Date:	Date:
Moon Phase: ○	Moon Phase: ○	Moon Phase: ○	Moon Phase: ○	Moon Phase: ○	Moon Phase: ○	Moon Phase: ○
Cycle Day:	Cycle Day:	Cycle Day:	Cycle Day:	Cycle Day:	Cycle Day:	Cycle Day:
Date:	Date:	Date:	Date:	Date:	Date:	Date:
Moon Phase: ○	Moon Phase: ○	Moon Phase: ○	Moon Phase: ○	Moon Phase: ○	Moon Phase: ○	Moon Phase: ○
Cycle Day:	Cycle Day:	Cycle Day:	Cycle Day:	Cycle Day:	Cycle Day:	Cycle Day:
Date:	Date:	Date:	Date:	Date:	Date:	Date:
Moon Phase: ○	Moon Phase: ○	Moon Phase: ○	Moon Phase: ○	Moon Phase: ○	Moon Phase: ○	Moon Phase: ○
Cycle Day:	Cycle Day:	Cycle Day:	Cycle Day:	Cycle Day:	Cycle Day:	Cycle Day:
Date:	Date:	Date:	Date:	Date:	Date:	Date:
Moon Phase: ○	Moon Phase: ○	Moon Phase: ○	Moon Phase: ○	Moon Phase: ○	Moon Phase: ○	Moon Phase: ○
Cycle Day:	Cycle Day:	Cycle Day:	Cycle Day:	Cycle Day:	Cycle Day:	Cycle Day:
Date:	Date:	Date:	Date:	Date:	Date:	Date:
Moon Phase: ○	Moon Phase: ○	Moon Phase: ○	Moon Phase: ○	Moon Phase: ○	Moon Phase: ○	Moon Phase: ○
Cycle Day:	Cycle Day:	Cycle Day:	Cycle Day:	Cycle Day:	Cycle Day:	Cycle Day:

Mapping my Moon

I move through my cycle with flow;
I feel my connections with the phases of the moon

Sunday	Monday	Tuesday	Wednesday	Thursday	Friday	Saturday
Date:	Date:	Date:	Date:	Date:	Date:	Date:
Moon Phase: ◯	Moon Phase: ◯	Moon Phase: ◯	Moon Phase: ◯	Moon Phase: ◯	Moon Phase: ◯	Moon Phase: ◯
Cycle Day:	Cycle Day:	Cycle Day:	Cycle Day:	Cycle Day:	Cycle Day:	Cycle Day:
Date:	Date:	Date:	Date:	Date:	Date:	Date:
Moon Phase: ◯	Moon Phase: ◯	Moon Phase: ◯	Moon Phase: ◯	Moon Phase: ◯	Moon Phase: ◯	Moon Phase: ◯
Cycle Day:	Cycle Day:	Cycle Day:	Cycle Day:	Cycle Day:	Cycle Day:	Cycle Day:
Date:	Date:	Date:	Date:	Date:	Date:	Date:
Moon Phase: ◯	Moon Phase: ◯	Moon Phase: ◯	Moon Phase: ◯	Moon Phase: ◯	Moon Phase: ◯	Moon Phase: ◯
Cycle Day:	Cycle Day:	Cycle Day:	Cycle Day:	Cycle Day:	Cycle Day:	Cycle Day:
Date:	Date:	Date:	Date:	Date:	Date:	Date:
Moon Phase: ◯	Moon Phase: ◯	Moon Phase: ◯	Moon Phase: ◯	Moon Phase: ◯	Moon Phase: ◯	Moon Phase: ◯
Cycle Day:	Cycle Day:	Cycle Day:	Cycle Day:	Cycle Day:	Cycle Day:	Cycle Day:
Date:	Date:	Date:	Date:	Date:	Date:	Date:
Moon Phase: ◯	Moon Phase: ◯	Moon Phase: ◯	Moon Phase: ◯	Moon Phase: ◯	Moon Phase: ◯	Moon Phase: ◯
Cycle Day:	Cycle Day:	Cycle Day:	Cycle Day:	Cycle Day:	Cycle Day:	Cycle Day:

Mapping my Moon

I move through my cycle with flow.
I feel my connections with the phases of the moon.

Sunday	Monday	Tuesday	Wednesday	Thursday	Friday	Saturday
Date:	Date:	Date:	Date:	Date:	Date:	Date:
Moon Phase: ○	Moon Phase: ○	Moon Phase: ○	Moon Phase: ○	Moon Phase: ○	Moon Phase: ○	Moon Phase: ○
Cycle Day:	Cycle Day:	Cycle Day:	Cycle Day:	Cycle Day:	Cycle Day:	Cycle Day:
Date:	Date:	Date:	Date:	Date:	Date:	Date:
Moon Phase: ○	Moon Phase: ○	Moon Phase: ○	Moon Phase: ○	Moon Phase: ○	Moon Phase: ○	Moon Phase: ○
Cycle Day:	Cycle Day:	Cycle Day:	Cycle Day:	Cycle Day:	Cycle Day:	Cycle Day:
Date:	Date:	Date:	Date:	Date:	Date:	Date:
Moon Phase: ○	Moon Phase: ○	Moon Phase: ○	Moon Phase: ○	Moon Phase: ○	Moon Phase: ○	Moon Phase: ○
Cycle Day:	Cycle Day:	Cycle Day:	Cycle Day:	Cycle Day:	Cycle Day:	Cycle Day:
Date:	Date:	Date:	Date:	Date:	Date:	Date:
Moon Phase: ○	Moon Phase: ○	Moon Phase: ○	Moon Phase: ○	Moon Phase: ○	Moon Phase: ○	Moon Phase: ○
Cycle Day:	Cycle Day:	Cycle Day:	Cycle Day:	Cycle Day:	Cycle Day:	Cycle Day:
Date:	Date:	Date:	Date:	Date:	Date:	Date:
Moon Phase: ○	Moon Phase: ○	Moon Phase: ○	Moon Phase: ○	Moon Phase: ○	Moon Phase: ○	Moon Phase: ○
Cycle Day:	Cycle Day:	Cycle Day:	Cycle Day:	Cycle Day:	Cycle Day:	Cycle Day:

Mapping my Moon

I move through my cycle with flow;
I feel my connections with the phases of the moon

Sunday	Monday	Tuesday	Wednesday	Thursday	Friday	Saturday
Date:	Date:	Date:	Date:	Date:	Date:	Date:
Moon Phase: ○	Moon Phase: ○	Moon Phase: ○	Moon Phase: ○	Moon Phase: ○	Moon Phase: ○	Moon Phase: ○
Cycle Day:	Cycle Day:	Cycle Day:	Cycle Day:	Cycle Day:	Cycle Day:	Cycle Day:
Date:	Date:	Date:	Date:	Date:	Date:	Date:
Moon Phase: ○	Moon Phase: ○	Moon Phase: ○	Moon Phase: ○	Moon Phase: ○	Moon Phase: ○	Moon Phase: ○
Cycle Day:	Cycle Day:	Cycle Day:	Cycle Day:	Cycle Day:	Cycle Day:	Cycle Day:
Date:	Date:	Date:	Date:	Date:	Date:	Date:
Moon Phase: ○	Moon Phase: ○	Moon Phase: ○	Moon Phase: ○	Moon Phase: ○	Moon Phase: ○	Moon Phase: ○
Cycle Day:	Cycle Day:	Cycle Day:	Cycle Day:	Cycle Day:	Cycle Day:	Cycle Day:
Date:	Date:	Date:	Date:	Date:	Date:	Date:
Moon Phase: ○	Moon Phase: ○	Moon Phase: ○	Moon Phase: ○	Moon Phase: ○	Moon Phase: ○	Moon Phase: ○
Cycle Day:	Cycle Day:	Cycle Day:	Cycle Day:	Cycle Day:	Cycle Day:	Cycle Day:
Date:	Date:	Date:	Date:	Date:	Date:	Date:
Moon Phase: ○	Moon Phase: ○	Moon Phase: ○	Moon Phase: ○	Moon Phase: ○	Moon Phase: ○	Moon Phase: ○
Cycle Day:	Cycle Day:	Cycle Day:	Cycle Day:	Cycle Day:	Cycle Day:	Cycle Day:

Mapping my Moon

I move through my cycle with flow;
I feel my connections with the phases of the moon

Sunday	Monday	Tuesday	Wednesday	Thursday	Friday	Saturday
Date:	Date:	Date:	Date:	Date:	Date:	Date:
Moon Phase: ○ Cycle Day:	Moon Phase: ○ Cycle Day:	Moon Phase: ○ Cycle Day:	Moon Phase: ○ Cycle Day:	Moon Phase: ○ Cycle Day:	Moon Phase: ○ Cycle Day:	Moon Phase: ○ Cycle Day:
Date:	Date:	Date:	Date:	Date:	Date:	Date:
Moon Phase: ○ Cycle Day:	Moon Phase: ○ Cycle Day:	Moon Phase: ○ Cycle Day:	Moon Phase: ○ Cycle Day:	Moon Phase: ○ Cycle Day:	Moon Phase: ○ Cycle Day:	Moon Phase: ○ Cycle Day:
Date:	Date:	Date:	Date:	Date:	Date:	Date:
Moon Phase: ○ Cycle Day:	Moon Phase: ○ Cycle Day:	Moon Phase: ○ Cycle Day:	Moon Phase: ○ Cycle Day:	Moon Phase: ○ Cycle Day:	Moon Phase: ○ Cycle Day:	Moon Phase: ○ Cycle Day:
Date:	Date:	Date:	Date:	Date:	Date:	Date:
Moon Phase: ○ Cycle Day:	Moon Phase: ○ Cycle Day:	Moon Phase: ○ Cycle Day:	Moon Phase: ○ Cycle Day:	Moon Phase: ○ Cycle Day:	Moon Phase: ○ Cycle Day:	Moon Phase: ○ Cycle Day:
Date:	Date:	Date:	Date:	Date:	Date:	Date:
Moon Phase: ○ Cycle Day:	Moon Phase: ○ Cycle Day:	Moon Phase: ○ Cycle Day:	Moon Phase: ○ Cycle Day:	Moon Phase: ○ Cycle Day:	Moon Phase: ○ Cycle Day:	Moon Phase: ○ Cycle Day:

Mapping my Moon

I move through my cycle with flow;
I feel my connections with the phases of the moon

Sunday	Monday	Tuesday	Wednesday	Thursday	Friday	Saturday
Date:	Date:	Date:	Date:	Date:	Date:	Date:
Moon Phase: ◯ Cycle Day:	Moon Phase: ◯ Cycle Day:	Moon Phase: ◯ Cycle Day:	Moon Phase: ◯ Cycle Day:	Moon Phase: ◯ Cycle Day:	Moon Phase: ◯ Cycle Day:	Moon Phase: ◯ Cycle Day:
Date:	Date:	Date:	Date:	Date:	Date:	Date:
Moon Phase: ◯ Cycle Day:	Moon Phase: ◯ Cycle Day:	Moon Phase: ◯ Cycle Day:	Moon Phase: ◯ Cycle Day:	Moon Phase: ◯ Cycle Day:	Moon Phase: ◯ Cycle Day:	Moon Phase: ◯ Cycle Day:
Date:	Date:	Date:	Date:	Date:	Date:	Date:
Moon Phase: ◯ Cycle Day:	Moon Phase: ◯ Cycle Day:	Moon Phase: ◯ Cycle Day:	Moon Phase: ◯ Cycle Day:	Moon Phase: ◯ Cycle Day:	Moon Phase: ◯ Cycle Day:	Moon Phase: ◯ Cycle Day:
Date:	Date:	Date:	Date:	Date:	Date:	Date:
Moon Phase: ◯ Cycle Day:	Moon Phase: ◯ Cycle Day:	Moon Phase: ◯ Cycle Day:	Moon Phase: ◯ Cycle Day:	Moon Phase: ◯ Cycle Day:	Moon Phase: ◯ Cycle Day:	Moon Phase: ◯ Cycle Day:
Date:	Date:	Date:	Date:	Date:	Date:	Date:
Moon Phase: ◯ Cycle Day:	Moon Phase: ◯ Cycle Day:	Moon Phase: ◯ Cycle Day:	Moon Phase: ◯ Cycle Day:	Moon Phase: ◯ Cycle Day:	Moon Phase: ◯ Cycle Day:	Moon Phase: ◯ Cycle Day:

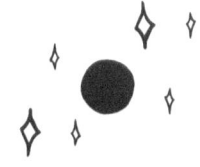

Mapping my Moon

I move through my cycle with flow;
I feel my connections with the phases of the moon

Sunday	Monday	Tuesday	Wednesday	Thursday	Friday	Saturday
Date:	Date:	Date:	Date:	Date:	Date:	Date:
Moon Phase: ○	Moon Phase: ○	Moon Phase: ○	Moon Phase: ○	Moon Phase: ○	Moon Phase: ○	Moon Phase: ○
Cycle Day:	Cycle Day:	Cycle Day:	Cycle Day:	Cycle Day:	Cycle Day:	Cycle Day:
Date:	Date:	Date:	Date:	Date:	Date:	Date:
Moon Phase: ○	Moon Phase: ○	Moon Phase: ○	Moon Phase: ○	Moon Phase: ○	Moon Phase: ○	Moon Phase: ○
Cycle Day:	Cycle Day:	Cycle Day:	Cycle Day:	Cycle Day:	Cycle Day:	Cycle Day:
Date:	Date:	Date:	Date:	Date:	Date:	Date:
Moon Phase: ○	Moon Phase: ○	Moon Phase: ○	Moon Phase: ○	Moon Phase: ○	Moon Phase: ○	Moon Phase: ○
Cycle Day:	Cycle Day:	Cycle Day:	Cycle Day:	Cycle Day:	Cycle Day:	Cycle Day:
Date:	Date:	Date:	Date:	Date:	Date:	Date:
Moon Phase: ○	Moon Phase: ○	Moon Phase: ○	Moon Phase: ○	Moon Phase: ○	Moon Phase: ○	Moon Phase: ○
Cycle Day:	Cycle Day:	Cycle Day:	Cycle Day:	Cycle Day:	Cycle Day:	Cycle Day:
Date:	Date:	Date:	Date:	Date:	Date:	Date:
Moon Phase: ○	Moon Phase: ○	Moon Phase: ○	Moon Phase: ○	Moon Phase: ○	Moon Phase: ○	Moon Phase: ○
Cycle Day:	Cycle Day:	Cycle Day:	Cycle Day:	Cycle Day:	Cycle Day:	Cycle Day:

Mapping my Moon

*I move through my cycle with flow;
I feel my connections with the phases of the moon*

Sunday	Monday	Tuesday	Wednesday	Thursday	Friday	Saturday
Date:	Date:	Date:	Date:	Date:	Date:	Date:
Moon Phase: ○ Cycle Day:	Moon Phase: ○ Cycle Day:	Moon Phase: ○ Cycle Day:	Moon Phase: ○ Cycle Day:	Moon Phase: ○ Cycle Day:	Moon Phase: ○ Cycle Day:	Moon Phase: ○ Cycle Day:
Date:	Date:	Date:	Date:	Date:	Date:	Date:
Moon Phase: ○ Cycle Day:	Moon Phase: ○ Cycle Day:	Moon Phase: ○ Cycle Day:	Moon Phase: ○ Cycle Day:	Moon Phase: ○ Cycle Day:	Moon Phase: ○ Cycle Day:	Moon Phase: ○ Cycle Day:
Date:	Date:	Date:	Date:	Date:	Date:	Date:
Moon Phase: ○ Cycle Day:	Moon Phase: ○ Cycle Day:	Moon Phase: ○ Cycle Day:	Moon Phase: ○ Cycle Day:	Moon Phase: ○ Cycle Day:	Moon Phase: ○ Cycle Day:	Moon Phase: ○ Cycle Day:
Date:	Date:	Date:	Date:	Date:	Date:	Date:
Moon Phase: ○ Cycle Day:	Moon Phase: ○ Cycle Day:	Moon Phase: ○ Cycle Day:	Moon Phase: ○ Cycle Day:	Moon Phase: ○ Cycle Day:	Moon Phase: ○ Cycle Day:	Moon Phase: ○ Cycle Day:
Date:	Date:	Date:	Date:	Date:	Date:	Date:
Moon Phase: ○ Cycle Day:	Moon Phase: ○ Cycle Day:	Moon Phase: ○ Cycle Day:	Moon Phase: ○ Cycle Day:	Moon Phase: ○ Cycle Day:	Moon Phase: ○ Cycle Day:	Moon Phase: ○ Cycle Day:

Mapping my Moon

*I move through my cycle with flow;
I feel my connections with the phases of the moon*

Sunday	Monday	Tuesday	Wednesday	Thursday	Friday	Saturday
Date:	Date:	Date:	Date:	Date:	Date:	Date:
Moon Phase: ○	Moon Phase: ○	Moon Phase: ○	Moon Phase: ○	Moon Phase: ○	Moon Phase: ○	Moon Phase: ○
Cycle Day:	Cycle Day:	Cycle Day:	Cycle Day:	Cycle Day:	Cycle Day:	Cycle Day:
Date:	Date:	Date:	Date:	Date:	Date:	Date:
Moon Phase: ○	Moon Phase: ○	Moon Phase: ○	Moon Phase: ○	Moon Phase: ○	Moon Phase: ○	Moon Phase: ○
Cycle Day:	Cycle Day:	Cycle Day:	Cycle Day:	Cycle Day:	Cycle Day:	Cycle Day:
Date:	Date:	Date:	Date:	Date:	Date:	Date:
Moon Phase: ○	Moon Phase: ○	Moon Phase: ○	Moon Phase: ○	Moon Phase: ○	Moon Phase: ○	Moon Phase: ○
Cycle Day:	Cycle Day:	Cycle Day:	Cycle Day:	Cycle Day:	Cycle Day:	Cycle Day:
Date:	Date:	Date:	Date:	Date:	Date:	Date:
Moon Phase: ○	Moon Phase: ○	Moon Phase: ○	Moon Phase: ○	Moon Phase: ○	Moon Phase: ○	Moon Phase: ○
Cycle Day:	Cycle Day:	Cycle Day:	Cycle Day:	Cycle Day:	Cycle Day:	Cycle Day:
Date:	Date:	Date:	Date:	Date:	Date:	Date:
Moon Phase: ○	Moon Phase: ○	Moon Phase: ○	Moon Phase: ○	Moon Phase: ○	Moon Phase: ○	Moon Phase: ○
Cycle Day:	Cycle Day:	Cycle Day:	Cycle Day:	Cycle Day:	Cycle Day:	Cycle Day:

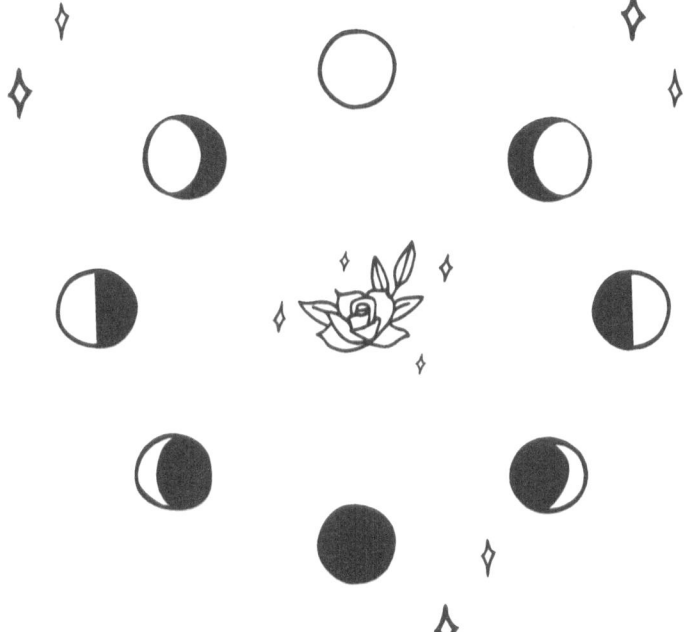

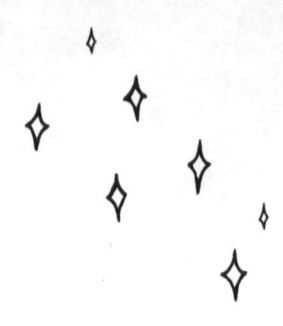

Infinite Flow

Accept and embrace.
Grow and change.
Not all is as it seems.
Surrender and open.

You are not the same person
as you were last year

You've listened.
You've answered honestly.
Your voice is louder.

You're moving through your life
with infinite flow.

With love and gratitude,

nikki

References and recommended reading:

Auset, Priestess Brandi, *The Goddess Guide: Exploring the Attributes and Correspondences of the Divine Feminine*. Minnesota Llewellyn Publications, 2017.

Askinosie, Heather and Jandro, Timmi, Crystal Muse: *Everyday Rituals to Tune to the Real You*. Hay House 2017.

Mildon, Emma, *Evolution of Goddess: A Modern Girl's Guide to Activating your Feminine Superpowers*. USA Enliven Books 2018.

About the Author

Nikki Tegg is a moon lover, stargazer, sacred space holder, reiki healer and mum. She also has a deep connection to the energies of the Goddess and Mother Earth. She nurtures creativity and shares her intuitive writing to empower women and other Goddesses.

Since her younger years, she's forever felt to be moving on a different plane, both energetically and spiritually, tuning into the signs and messages around her and embracing natural clairvoyant and clairsentient abilities. Nikki's fascination with the stars and moon have led the way to her spiritual awakening, where she surrenders in trust to the Universe, giving voice to her psychic mediumship and intuitive prose. Nikki provides soulful guidance through connection to Spirit to empower others on their life path. She loves all things Goddess and bringing women together in sisterhood, for connection and healing through sacred circles.

www.ingramcontent.com/pod-product-compliance
Lightning Source LLC
Chambersburg PA
CBHW020322010526
44107CB00054B/1939